Home Start
*supporting families*

# CHANGE LIVES
## IN NORTHERN IRELAND

Home Start
*supporting families*

# CHANGING LIVES

## IN NORTHERN IRELAND

STORIES COMPILED BY **HEATHER CAMERON**

EDITOR **WENDY DICKINSON**

FAMILY LIAISON **RUTH WEIR**

vodafone™
UK FOUNDATION

THIS BOOK HAS BEEN MADE POSSIBLE THROUGH THE GENEROUS SUPPORT OF THE VODAFONE UK FOUNDATION

PUBLISHED BY **HOME-START**. WWW.HOME-START.ORG.UK

First published in 2005 by Home-Start
2 Salisbury Road
Leicester
LE1 7QR

0116 233 9955
www.home-start.org.uk

Photography : **David Austin**
Jay Neilly
John Taggart

Printed in Great Britain

ISBN  0-9508349-3-9

**Thanks to all the families, volunteers and staff who contributed to this book and particularly to Margaret Thompson and her team at Home-Start Antrim for their help with photography.**

# FOREWORD

When I first heard about Home-Start I felt real empathy for the families and volunteers involved. As a father myself – and one of five brothers – I know from personal experience about the pressures facing families today.

The reality is that any family, wherever they are and whatever their circumstances, can sometimes find it difficult to cope alone. That's where the very special parent-to-parent support offered by Home-Start comes in.

It makes sense, doesn't it? Who do you go to when you need advice and support? People who've been there, done it, got the t-shirt, of course.

But not everyone has family and friends to lean on, and that's where Home-Start is doing such a great job, helping thousands of children and their parents every year.

This collection of very personal stories, written by families and volunteers, speak eloquently of the powerful, life-changing effect of Home-Start. Such stories of empowerment and positive change are being lived out in Northern Ireland and across the UK on a daily basis.

In reading *Home-Start – Changing Lives in Northern Ireland*, I'm sure you will want to do more to ensure that the Home-Start story can be told in every community, so that parents and their children can be supported towards independence and a brighter future.

**Eamonn Holmes**

# HOME-START

Home-Start has a powerful impact on the lives of thousands of children and parents every day, offering family support that cuts across all boundaries – of sex, social class, ethnic origin and financial status.

Parent volunteers visit families with young children, at home, to offer friendship, practical help and emotional support.

But why do families need Home-Start?

In an ideal world Home-Start wouldn't exist – friends, relations and communities would support those young families who, for a variety of reasons, sometimes find it hard to cope with the problems life throws at them.

But the reality is that more and more families are turning to Home-Start every day as the pressures on family life – poverty, income inequality, stress, isolation, loneliness and mental and physical illness – increase.

Home-Start's local Schemes are rooted in the communities they serve, managed locally by volunteer trustees and supported by the national charity to ensure consistent and quality support for children and parents, wherever they are, and whatever their circumstances.

Home-Start's vision is a society in which every parent has the support they need to give their children the best possible start in life.

Our goal is to have support available in every community in the UK.

**For more information about Home-Start, to find out about becoming a volunteer or to make a donation call our free information line :
08000 68 63 68**

# A MOTHER'S STORY

**Karen**

**I am a mother of five children** ranging in age from fourteen years (with attitude and boys on the brain) to ten months (a baby with truly awesome limpet-like qualities). I am putting a twelve-year-old abusive marriage with an alcoholic husband to bed, trying to build a relationship with a new partner and in a new house while having started a new family (not the easiest activity at 38).

Hating myself has become such a permanent feature that I scarcely notice it anymore. The only thing that can vary is what I do about it. Sometimes I'll hurt myself until I feel better, other times I will be a Grade A bitch and try to hurt everyone around me. I can curl up, ignore the world (partner, children, dog and hamster) and wait to die or I can paper over the cracks, let on I'm ok and take some pills. Being on my own in the house with the kids can leave me feeling quite isolated but knowing that I'm going to be paralysed by a panic attack two minutes after leaving my front door means that I need my hand held nearly everywhere I go.

Last February, after the birth of my youngest child, my health visitor felt that I might benefit from some help with the children. Take a mother's natural protectiveness to her new child and magnify it by your telephone number (including std code) and you will see that there's no way this lady's going to let her kids go anywhere to give her a break. However, she did have an option of which I had previously been unaware: Home-Start. I was referred and shortly thereafter I had a call from Eelco, a Home-Start manager, asking to come round and see me. You've got to love this guy; he brings his own biscuits. For the price of a cup of tea he had my life story, background, needs and short-term goals in a gift-wrapped package. Surprisingly, he did not have a vast pool of

## KAREN, A MOTHER.
## HOME-START EAST BELFAST

bodies which he could draw on at random to knock on my door once a week and ask how I was. Instead, Eelco left with the promise that he would now begin the search for a volunteer who was suitable, had similar life experience, likes and dislikes. Some chance!

A few weeks later Eelco called to say that he had found a volunteer who he thought might be right for me. God help her. The next day he called with Eithne, a girl of my age who had kids and had done so many similar things to me that it was uncanny (no biscuits this time though). Eelco left us chatting, small talk a prelude to the serious business of getting to know one another. Over several weeks we met at the house; Eithne helping me with the every day needs of the children and prising me out of the house like a snail from its shell. Short walks to the shop and local

For the price of a cup of tea he had my life story, background, needs and short-term goals in a gift-wrapped package.

cafes laid the foundation to building general interests which involved both of us. We joined a gym at which we take great delight in afflicting the maximum amount of damage on ourselves and have recently started an evening foundation course in counselling (I'm learning to help people? go figure).

Eithne wasn't just a girl who called once a week, though. Possibly the most important aspect of her friendship and mentoring was that she was always willing to listen to my ups and downs no matter what her own problems were at the time.

**Karen with her daughter**

Through the support of Home-Start and the friendship of people like Eithne and Eelco I have achieved many of my short-term goals and more besides. I've found myself making progress in areas that I hadn't dared think I could have addressed before. I still have bad days but now I have more good days and look forward to better days. My quality of life has improved and I've made the move from being an out and out pessimist to being an optimist with experience. Eelco asked me to write about my experiences with Home-Start but I also want to take the opportunity to thank them for their care and support at a time when I needed it most, and for finding me a new friend.

My name is Emma and I'm a Home-Start volunteer. I'm married to Alan and we have two beautiful children, Alana, aged five and three-year-old Brandon. My first contact with Home-Start was when I was referred by my Health Visitor in 2001. Soon after my son was born I had postnatal depression, which left me feeling very lonely and isolated, especially since I live in the country and at the time didn't drive.

When I was told what Home-Start did I felt a bit funny about having a stranger coming into my home, but soon after meeting my volunteer, Gladys. I soon changed my mind as she was so kind and warm towards my children and myself. Gladys became my friend and became almost like a grandmother to my little ones. Gladys was my volunteer for six months and in those six months I learned how to enjoy parenthood instead of seeing it as something which I couldn't cope with.

I was so influenced by the good work of Home-Start that when my little girl started school in 2003 I decided to volunteer and soon I was starting my training course, though I must admit I was feeling very nervous.

I'm now a volunteer to two families who have very different needs. My families are lovely and I've made really good friendships with them. I have to say that when I leave their homes I've got a warm feeling inside just knowing that I've been able to help others by my experiences in the past.

Home-Start has given me confidence that I didn't know was possible. I've made so many friends its almost like being accepted into an extended family where everyone is made to feel welcome.

In the near future I would like to pursue a career in social work and I think Home-Start will help me towards this. For right now I'm really happy being with Home-Start.

# EMMA
## A VOLUNTEER

## HOME-START
## CAUSEWAY

# PAYING IT FORWARD...

**David**

I am 47 and live along the beautiful North Antrim Coast of Northern Ireland. I am the father of two beautiful children – Rachael, 17 and Christopher, 14, whom I love dearly. Unfortunately my marriage has ended. I served in the Police Service of Northern Ireland for 18 years but was medically retired two years ago due to an injury at work. Almost five years of separation, and no longer working, made me feel socially devalued. My self-esteem was low, and I was on anti-depressants. One day I saw a sign for Causeway Volunteer Bureau, in my hometown of Coleraine, Northern Ireland and they had lots of suggestions – Riding for the Disabled, Hospice Driver, a volunteer with Causeway Home-Start. I said YES to all three, and left with the joys of Spring in my step, even though it was Summer.

No sooner had I got back home then the phone rang. It was the Causeway Home-Start organiser, Ann Laird. Like most of us from this side of the ocean, she has a bit of the Blarney in her. I was taken by her words. Half an hour later she was at my door. I panicked when the doorbell rang, as I had quite a mountain of ironing to do, but the wonders of a cup of tea and a Wagon Wheel! It did the trick as she laughed to calm me down saying, 'It is a bit messy in this house (I had three 14-year-old boys staying over from the night before), but it is a home!' I felt part of a family immediately. Something I much needed, and I gladly accepted her invitation on to a Preparation Course.

I felt excited, anxious, but more importantly included. I never felt different being a male (apart from some brief moments when I had to stare embarrassingly at the ceiling when one lady happened to tell a joke about bottle feeding... ahem!)

## DAVID, A VOLUNTEER.
## HOME-START CAUSEWAY

I'm now waiting for a family placement but I have been elected on to the Management Committee as Minute Secretary and have been offering my time for jobs around the office. I've learned to gloss paint the front door, paint and stencil the toilet, and even replace a carpet. First I had to haggle with a local carpet store, then drive around the town with four large rolls sticking out of my car window getting some strange looks, then had to replace the toilet seat with a new wooden one, having broken the plastic one whilst trying to stencil, and nearly trapping my foot in the U bend…

All very Home-Start! What have I got out of it? A sense of purpose. 'Paying it forward' so to speak, and in this small way making it spread, in the same way that it came to me. I have made new friendships and it was a lovely feeling all round, being wanted … and my self-esteem is back!

**David with his son Christopher**

# THE ONE CONSTANT SOURCE OF SECURITY IN A CHILD'S LIFE

**ELIZABETH, A VOLUNTEER. HOME-START BALLYNAHINCH**

I first heard of Home-Start when I was doing a course at Belfast Bible College and one day an elderly student was describing four children in her life.

Two of these children were living in Nepal with no running water, no electricity, no local hospital etc: the other two were living in her home town in Northern Ireland with all the seeming advantages of 21st century life.

Yet it was these last two children that this woman was most concerned about. It turned out that the children in Nepal were her grandchildren and part of a loving, secure family. The other two are in her Home-Start family, where she is a home-visiting volunteer, and life for them is very unstable because of all sorts of difficulties. She, the volunteer, was the one constant source of security in the lives of these children.

When I later noticed the Home-Start sign in Ballynahinch I made enquiries, trained, got my first family and now I am with family number three. I volunteered because I felt, as a mother of twenty years standing, that I had something to offer young families who are finding life a bit of a struggle.

I remember the days when my husband had taken the car to work, it was raining so hard I didn't want to take the children out for a walk because we would all be soaked and I just longed for a friend or

neighbour to call in for a chat. Life with small children can be quite isolating.

I am loving my experience of being a Home-Start volunteer. I have had three families so far, all with different circumstances and needs. With one family I have been storyteller, picnic organiser, piano player for musical games, swing-pusher and very often battle referee (three boys very close together!).

With another I am mum's chief listener and encourager. It is so rewarding to see someone who has been crippled by post-natal depression beginning to take an active part in family and community life again.

With my third family my frugal nature is coming to the fore as I help mum and her partner, on a very small income, shop for and learn to cook nutritious, economical meals. Little tips and lessons on how to light a fire with newspaper and sticks instead of firelighters, or how a brisk walk can lift your mood, have been very well received.

Volunteering with Home-Start has been a very good move for me. It makes me feel that my experience of being a mother can be passed on. I have also shared in the lives of people I wouldn't normally meet and I feel it is such a privilege to be welcomed into their homes and to be included almost as part of the family.

## Life with small children can be quite isolating.

# FINDING A VERY SPECIAL FRIEND...

**HEATHER, A MOTHER.**
**HOME-START NEWRY**

My name is Heather and I am a Mum of triplets – two boys and a girl. They were born on the 17th March, 2001 and all healthy. They were in incubators for almost three weeks. Steven was 4lbs 2oz, Darren 3lbs 7oz and Lauren 3lbs 8oz. My husband took a few days off work when the babies came home. I was in hospital myself for ten weeks previous to the birth and I too was glad to come home.

My husband had to go back to work and I found myself looking at three babies and all needing feeding. My life was very hectic and days and nights were the same. I had no time for myself. The babies fed quite frequently and very slowly, so one feed ran onto the next feed.

This was so hard and I never expected it to be so time consuming. Very soon I became very exhausted and quite ill. I never felt depressed but just had the feelings of running away.

A month after contacting Home-Start they found a volunteer for me. This was great. Rita started the following week. When she came I hugged her and I just gave her a baby to feed. We started chatting and feeding babies. I have made a very special friend; I never called Rita a volunteer… always a friend. She gave me the opportunity to do what I liked for the time she was there. I often went for a bath or went to my bedroom and just chilled out with soft music. I never went too far in case Rita needed me but three years on now and Rita still comes to my need.

**Heather and David with their triplets,
(left to right) Steven, Lauren & Darren**

Things have got much easier now and Rita has taught me to be relaxed and enjoy life. I have learnt so much from her. Most of all Steven, Darren and Lauren love her and just have to see her every week.

I dedicate this story to Rita.

I was suffering from depression and my health visitor thought I needed the support of someone coming in on a regular basis who understood what I was going through. Initially I didn't want someone coming into my home because I felt they would be watching everything I did and I would feel uncomfortable with someone I didn't know. I decided I would try Home-Start before taking any alternative steps of support that were offered. Now that my volunteer is coming every week I wouldn't be without her. She is caring and friendly and easy to talk to. She is attentive to my needs and shares her experiences of child development, which I appreciate as a first time mum.

# FIONA
## A MOTHER

## HOME-START
## CRAIGAVON

# HOW A STRANGER BECOMES PART OF YOUR LIFE...

**LINDA, A MOTHER &
JESS, HER HOME-START
VOLUNTEER. HOME-START
CAUSEWAY**

## Linda's story

After the birth of my fourth child in 2001, my health visitor suggested that she may be able to get me some help from a Home-Start volunteer. As I am taking a lot of medication for many health problems and I was recovering from a Caesarean birth, I was finding it hard to cope with a new baby. I have three other children, then aged 9, 7 and 18 months. My husband was off work for six months with back problems so I was finding it hard to cope with everything going on in my life.

When my health visitor first suggested a volunteer from Home-Start I was unsure about it, as I had never heard of it before. I didn't know if I would really want a stranger coming into my house. Little did I think then that this person would make such a difference and become part of my family.

Often, when Jess, my volunteer called, we just talked or she played with the children, sometimes taking them to the park. A few months later we moved house and Jess came on the day we moved, giving up her day to help us. She rolled up her sleeves and helped in whatever way she could. The house we moved in to was in bad order. We needed a kitchen and she said she could get someone to put one in for is, meaning her husband. He gave up his Saturdays to help us put in a new kitchen.

**Left to right: Linda, Laura-Jayne (3), Mark (5) and Jess**

Later in the year she asked me if I could manage to go away with her on holiday for a week to give me a break away from all that was going on at the time and to give me some time on my own without the children. We set off in July for Spain for a week. I was unsure of the travelling and how it would affect my health. My husband was very good and took a week off work to look after the children. It was the best thing I have done. The heat was very good for me and eased my pains and I haven't felt as well in years. It also gave me a lot of confidence. Going away was such a lovely experience, and having time to myself. It was lovely having someone to listen to me and talk with. I had such a lovely time and it was one of the best weeks of my life.

From my own experience with Home-Start, I can't recommend it enough or thank them enough for the difference it has made to my life and my family.

# Jess's story

I have been a Home-Start volunteer since it was first established in my area in 1995. I was then part of a group of ten women who met weekly in a small cramped office to be trained as the first group of volunteers in the Causeway area. At that time, my children were well settled into school routine and I felt I wanted to do something worthwhile and interesting with my free mornings.

**Laura-Jayne (3) and Mark (5)**

Since then I have worked with several families, all very different and having different needs. My first family involved visiting a home where the mother was suffering from ME and found it difficult to get through the daily routine with her children. Thankfully she has now fully recovered from her illness and runs her own business. Over the years we have developed a close friendship and still keep in regular contact with each other.

I have also visited a family for some time whose baby has a similar special needs condition to that of my own daughter. This was a very special family to go into as it reminded me of the situation I was in the year previous. Again it was often just listening to the mother and answering questions about my own experience. Although I no longer call as a volunteer, I still see the family and hear how things are going for them.

At present I am with a family where the mother has been suffering from many physical problems over the years. This means taking a lot of medication, which leaves her tired and struggling to cope with the demands of four young children. On top of all the pressures of the daily routine she was on the verge of moving house to the country. This meant packing up and trying to settle into a new life for the whole family, which was a difficult time for them. In the summer she and I had a week's holiday in Spain. Her husband very kindly took time off work to look after the children. It was a lovely experience for both of us as we so enjoyed each other's company and had time to talk without constantly considering the children.

I have gained a great deal as a volunteer and hope that families whom I have visited and grown to know have found it as worthwhile as I have.

# SIOBHAN
## A VOLUNTEER

## HOME-START
## CLOGHER VALLEY

When I first saw an ad for Home-Start about six years ago in my local paper, I thought what a good idea it was but at that time I still had a young family and enough problems of my own to keep me going. After the new Clogher Valley Scheme organiser, also called Siobhan, took up post I joined the committee to help get it up and running in the area. As it is a rural area and this idea was very new this was a mammoth task. I went on to join the Scheme's first volunteer preparation course and this was followed shortly afterwards by my first family.

About the same time I had just completed a Diploma in Community Development, with hopes of furthering myself in the employment field. After a few disappointments my hopes were soon dropped and my spirits low.

Then one day Siobhan called me to say a local Home-Start Scheme was looking for a temporary organiser to cover sick leave. I jumped at the chance even though the contract was only for three months. I couldn't believe it when I was told I got the job. At first the job sounded daunting as the scheme had been without an organiser for a number of months, but with the help of other organisers, a very strong committee, regional consultant, a great bunch of volunteers and of course Anne, Scheme secretary (my right hand woman) I managed to get things going again. My three months turned into a year and by that time the Scheme managed to secure quite a large amount of much needed funding and new volunteers were recruited and trained. Just as the organiser was ready to come back I succeeded to get a job as a family participation worker, with thanks to Home-Start.

*Siobhan McIlroy is now a member of staff at Home-Start West Tyrone*

# WHEN A CHILD TELLS YOU HE LOVES YOU

**PHILIPPA, A VOLUNTEER.**
**HOME-START NORTH DOWN**

I chose to give up my career in 1990 on the birth of my first child. Subsequently I spent eleven years as a full time parent to three children. I largely enjoyed this time. As any parent knows, caring for children is extremely rewarding, but it can also be very demanding, often lonely and at times downright boring!

Eventually, as my children grew older, I became aware that parenting on its own was not enough to make me feel completely fulfilled as a person. I felt it was time to put some feelers out into the 'real' world, but I lacked the experience and the confidence to apply for employment. I wanted to do something that would not only be useful to others, but also help me regain my self-confidence and feel valuable as a member of society.

Home-Start appealed to me more than other organisations because it is a charity devoted to the family. I felt I had a great deal of experience in this and therefore something to offer.

I have no female relatives living in this country and in the past I have suffered from post-natal depression. There were times, particularly when my two older children were smaller, that I longed for both practical and emotional support. I felt that if I could be of help to just one other person in a similar position then it was well worth doing.

It was with some trepidation that I attended the Home-Start volunteer training course. I immediately felt at ease as, under the guidelines of our Home-Start co-ordinator, we bounced ideas off one another and questioned our values and attitudes. At the end of the nine week course, I not only felt ready to support my first family, but I had also made some good friends.

When I met my first family, I quickly warmed to both the mother and the children. Naomi, our Home-Start Organiser, appears to have an uncanny knack of matching the right volunteer with the right family. Although I was initially there to give practical help, it soon became apparent that the mother needed emotional support as well. It took some months for her to talk about this, but when she finally did, it really felt like a breakthrough. Not only did the mother and I become friends, but also, as our youngest children are similar in age, so did our families. I visited this family for two-and-a-half years before they

## As a Home-Start volunteer, I never feel isolated

felt they no longer needed a Home-Start volunteer. We plan to keep in touch. Naomi has just recently placed me with my second family.

As a Home-Start volunteer, I never feel isolated. I feel as though I am part of a team and know that if I encounter any difficulties I can contact my Home-Start Organiser at any time for support. There are also monthly support meetings where we have the opportunity to meet with other volunteers and receive regular training. I have found being a volunteer for Home-Start an extremely positive experience.

**Philippa**

The most obvious reward is the sense of helping people. Being a volunteer can occasionally be emotionally draining, but there are also poignant moments; for example when a child in your Home-Start family tells you he loves you, or the mother says she doesn't know how she would manage without you, it feels wonderful. It is a privilege to have the opportunity to build a relationship with a family and watch that relationship develop, and although there can be a feeling of sadness when you leave a family who no longer need you, the sense of achievement is second to none.

Another plus point has been the social aspect of Home-Start. I have thoroughly enjoyed meeting other volunteers and making friends. I have also gained enormously from the training course such as 'First Aid for Children' and 'The Importance of Play'. These have been valuable to me not only in my role as Home-Start volunteer, but also in my role as parent.

On a more personal level, Home-Start was something of a springboard for me. My experience as a volunteer has helped me to feel as though I do have something to offer to society and has given me the self-confidence I needed to take another step and complete a computer course. This in turn increased my confidence to the extent that I felt able to seek employment, something that would have been unthinkable to me four years ago! I believe that the excellent training I received from Home-Start helped me to achieve this goal and I now work as a part-time Community Care Worker for a local charity. This allows me to feel fulfilled and at the same time continue to be at home for my children and carry on as a volunteer for Home-Start.

## EMMA
### A MOTHER
### HOME-START CRAIGAVON

My Home-Start volunteer Joan is brilliant with the children and very inventive where games are concerned. She is also a great listener who I find very easy to talk to. We are hoping to go together to a community house that deals with parenting issues. I have wanted to for a long time but lacked the courage to go alone. Now that I know Joan can go with me I am really looking forward to it and will hopefully meet some other parents who may be in a situation similar to mine.

## MARGARET
### A VOLUNTEER
### HOME-START ANTRIM

I worked as a nurse for 26 years and had to take early retirement due to ill health. My girls were growing up quickly and didn't depend on me as much. I thought, 'what do I do next?' I muddled through for two years until a friend introduced me to Home-Start. If I'm honest I had never heard of it and wondered what could it offer me as a volunteer. What had I got to lose?

I was introduced to the Scheme manager who supported and encouraged me and convinced me that I had something I could give to families who needed that extra bit of help and support with their young children, whatever their problems might be. I have been a volunteer for three years now and have supported two families, both long term, and I also help with the weekly family morning group.

A lot has happened in my own personal life in the last two years and I know that without being involved in Home-Start I would not have got through it. It has given me a purpose in life – a reason to get up in the morning. I have made many new friends but most of all I must say thank you to Home-Start, you really have changed my life!

# "ALONG THE WAY JOY BECAME MY FRIEND, NOT JUST A VOLUNTEER"

## ...HOW A FAMILY TRAGEDY LED TO A DEEP FRIENDSHIP

**PAULINE & JOY'S STORY.**
**HOME-START**
**DOWN DISTRICT**

## Pauline's story

My name is Pauline. Three and a half years ago my husband was killed by a drunk driver. He simply went to work and never came back. I was devastated. The police came to my house in the early hours of the morning to tell me the news and I thought it was a bad dream. How would I tell my three young children that Daddy wasn't coming home? At the time my son was six and my twin daughters only three. I immediately plunged into the depths of depression mixed with shock and disbelief, how could this possibly happen to us, why my family?

I got a visit from Lila, the Home-Start Organiser for my area, in the middle of December and we discussed getting a volunteer. Soon after I was introduced to Joy. We had a lot in common, the main thing being that she was a widow and knew exactly what I was going through – the feelings I was experiencing, the sometimes mad thoughts that I was having. She never thought they we mad but reassured me that it was all part of what we were going through.

The trust developed quite quickly between us, with Joy supporting me in numerous ways; helping with the children, being an extra pair of hands when the children were off school, practical things that I had taken for granted before but that became massive mountains to climb when you're suddenly left on your own.

**Pauline and Joy**

Slowly the mountains became smaller, the unsolvable problems became solvable again, and slowly but surely I began to see the light at the end of the tunnel that I was trapped in. Joy helped me to see it. She became the listening ear that I so desperately needed. Joy became my lifeline. I can remember watching the clock until she would knock on the door.

Joy always had confidence in me that I didn't have. She knew that I would cope even when I thought I'd never cope with anything ever again. When the court process started to convict my husband's killer, I thought I would never get through it but I did with Joy's help. Somewhere along the way, Joy became my friend and not just a volunteer. Looking back over the last few years, I know I could have never made it through without Joy's help.

**Jack**

Even though Joy no longer visits me as a volunteer, there is one thing I'm absolutely sure of, we will always be good friends. Home-Start is a much-needed service to a lot of people with varied problems. Sometimes it is difficult to ask for help, or even recognise that you need it, but everyone could use a shoulder to lean on when times are tough.

Thank you, Joy for being my shoulder.

## Joy's story

In 1998, having worked for many years as a nurse in my local hospital, I was forced to take early retirement due to ill health. Two years later, with my health greatly improved, I found myself with nothing to do, feeling rather useless and sinking deeper into the proverbial rut. I was determined to pull myself together and find something useful to do. Soon after, I saw a notice in the local paper looking for volunteers for Home-Start. At that time I had only vaguely heard of the organisation, and had no idea what it did. However the notice in the paper gave sufficient information to make me want to find out more about it. The fact that it involved working with families with young children and that there was a training course to be undertaken first, really appealed to me. I duly rang up Lila, the organiser of the local Home-Start Scheme, who came out to see me to explain about Home-Start's work. Lila was so nice and so enthusiastic that I was hooked, and enrolled for the next Volunteer Preparation Course due to start in two weeks time. It was really interesting and as well as preparing me for volunteering, it gave me the chance to make new friends and feel that I 'belonged' to something again.

## …it gave me the chance to make new friends and feel that I 'belonged' to something again.

Lila matched me with a family three days before Christmas 2000, almost immediately after our preparation course had finished. I was really nervous the first time I visited Pauline on my own, as she had lots of problems; she had very poor health herself, a son of six and twin daughters of three, one of

**Joy and Pauline**

whom had an autistic spectrum disorder. Worst of all, her beloved husband had recently been knocked down and killed by a drunk driver. He had cared for her when she was sick, as well as the children, and had always been a tremendous support to her. It was thus a very daunting prospect, as I wondered how on earth I was going to be able to comfort and support this young woman, who had experienced such tragedy in her life. However, I knew that Lila had matched me with her as I too had experienced the loss of my husband several years before, from cancer; also my eldest son had been born with severe brain damage, so I understood about rearing a child with a disability.

I needn't have worried; Pauline and I took to each other straight away, and felt able to talk freely to each other. When, after my third visit she eagerly asked me if I would be going the next week, it's hard to explain what a good feeling it gave me to know that she liked me and wanted me to keep visiting her. I knew then that I must have been doing

**Jack, Mollie & Taylor**

something right! Most of my visits were spent with Pauline talking and listening. She didn't have anyone else to confide in and really needed to be able to talk to someone, safe in the knowledge that it was completely confidential and that I would never talk about what we discussed. I felt very privileged to know that she trusted me with her confidences.

Some days we would go out to the shops or just into town for a coffee. In the holidays we would take the children to the playground in the park. I really enjoyed getting to know the children and it was a great feeling when the children got to know me, running up to me when I arrived; or sometimes when I was in the town I would hear my name called and I would see the children waving at me from the car. I learnt how to handle Mollie, the twin with mild autism, and was rewarded when she would come and sit on my knee, as she would be very wary of most people.

The children are now past the age for Home-Start volunteer support, but Pauline and I have become such good friends that I still call and see her and the children regularly and she will phone me if anything important is happening. Although I know that life will never be the same for Pauline and her children, I find it very rewarding to see the changes in her, as she worked through her grief and came out of the shadows, and found ways to cope with her life.

I now have two other families whom I visit regularly, and I really enjoy my visits. I find that each family has different needs so you need to be flexible as a Home-Start volunteer.

I definitely think that joining Home-Start is the best thing I have done. It has given me a sense of purpose and the great feeling that I am doing something worthwhile.

# MARGARET

## A VOLUNTEER

## HOME-START
## ANTRIM

It was the Christmas before last as I was making my way through the Castle Centre in Antrim, that I came upon a jovial group of Home-Start people. I gave them a donation and was asked if I would consider being a volunteer.

Some weeks later I decided to apply and was warmly accepted as part of the Home-Start Antrim team. The first thing I noticed was how friendly the atmosphere was and how well everyone was treated. My experience during the introductory course was one of acceptance as part of one big happy family. I was impressed by the courses on offer, which were all very professional and of the highest standard, so you are learning all the time as well as doing some good for the community. My first six months or so have been completed as a first–time volunteer and I am pleased that things are going really well. So, in this cynical dog-eat-dog world, it is gratifying to know that there is a body of people, quietly getting on with being a positive force for good in the community. My own two girls have grown up and one is a mum herself. Home-Start has changed my life and given it direction. I, for one, am very proud to be counted amongst their ranks and am grateful to them for a chance to follow in their footsteps.

## A VOLUNTEER

## HOME-START
## ANTRIM

I joined Home-Start after losing my mum, who was not only my mum but also my best friend. I felt very lost as all my time had been spent with my mum. After volunteering with Home-Start I made many new friends who all cared. I was given a family to visit and felt needed again. The mum of the family I visited lost her mum, dad and best friend all inside eight months. I was there for her and felt I could give her comfort and perhaps know a little of what she was feeling. I love my work with Home-Start and it has really changed my life.

# WORKING TO CHANGE LIVES FOR THE BETTER

**Margaret with 8 week old Bethany, granddaughter of volunteer, Carmel**

I first heard about Home-Start in September 1987. My youngest child's nursery school teacher suggested I might have some time on my hands and like to join a new voluntary organisation starting in North Belfast where I live. They were looking for parents to share their experience of bringing up their families, to help support other parents.

After being at home with our six children for so many years, it was a bit daunting trying something new, but I went along and met Hilary Smith, the organiser of this new idea.

I needn't have worried, from day one I realised this organisation was very friendly, welcoming and although we didn't actually know this term in 1987, very "inclusive".

I visited many families over the next three years, with a whole range of needs. My first family had very premature triplets, needing a lot of attention. First time parents and quite young, they did a brilliant job. When I see the triplets now doing their GCSEs my heart gives a little flutter.

Home-Start in the late 1980s consisted of one scheme in East Belfast and one in North Belfast…by 1990 there were five schemes and another one planned for Antrim.

## MARGARET THOMPSON, ORGANISER.
## HOME-START ANTRIM

I was encouraged to apply for the position of organiser in Antrim. I did, and surprisingly enough (to me anyway) I got the job. That was fourteen years ago and I'm still here (some might say "Have you no ambition?") but I love working for Home-Start, the families, the volunteers, the other schemes – it has all been very rewarding.

Over the years I have met many, many people and made friends that have lasted nearly two decades.

I didn't see my life going in this direction 20 years ago, I was thinking of becoming a wedding planner (only joking) – no, I was going to do interior design and set up my own business, but as I look back I'm very glad I didn't. I have grown emotionally over the years, I have never regretted being a part of Home-Start. I believe in the idea, the simple philosophy of sharing experiences with others. It can change lives for the better.

Over the years I have met many, many people and made friends that have lasted nearly two decades.

# "I HAVE CRIED WITH THEM AND I'VE LAUGHED WITH THEM..."

**CARMEL, VOLUNTEER.
HOME-START ANTRIM**

We arrived in Antrim 27 years ago – my husband, our three-week-old twin daughters and myself. I was originally from a small village in Donegal, where I knew everyone, and my husband was from Belfast. In Antrim we lived in a small estate which was close to the town. My husband had a full time job. Our house, although we hadn't much in it, was comfortable and we had two beautiful children. Even though I had so much, to this day I will never forget how alone and lonely I was and even though there was a lot of people and houses around me, I had never felt so isolated in all my life.

Another two children and sixteen years on, when my children were all now at school and again feeling lonely and with spare time on my hands, I saw an advertisement in our local paper looking for volunteers for Home-Start – 'parents helping parents'. I knew at once I fitted the bill. So I joined Home-Start and became a volunteer. Eleven years on I am still volunteering – with a break in-between when I had a little late bundle of joy myself. Needless to say I hadn't a lot of time to volunteer with a little one about.

I became a volunteer with Home-Start first and foremost because I never forgot how I felt when I arrived in Antrim all those years ago. Knowing about the good work that Home-Start does, how I wish it had been in Antrim when I arrived with my twin daughters.

**Carmel with 3 of her grandchildren, Nieve (18 months), Bethany (8 weeks) and Leah (also 18 months)**

I also love working with children and I thought if I could give a parent who was feeling lonely, stressed, isolated or who just needs a chat with someone, a break for an hour or two every week then I knew from my own experience that volunteering for Home-Start would be worthwhile.

Over the years I have volunteered with many families, all different in their own way but with one common bond, they just needed someone to talk to, to be there for them. I have shared a lot of experiences with my families. I have cried with them and I have laughed with them. I have made firm friends with some of them and remain so to this day. Sometimes its so hard to move on and leave your family when you are no longer needed, likewise it is nerve-wracking but also exciting when you go to meet your new family for the first time. For me, being a volunteer with Home-Start has been an enriching and rewarding experience. What better reward than to watch a mother grow strong in confidence and self-esteem or seeing children coming out of their shells and all this because I go to visit a family for a couple of hours a week, may it be to chat to a mother or to play with the children while the mother gets a well earned and much needed break. How humble I feel to be allowed to do this knowing that they do not feel threatened by

**Leah**

**Carmel's granddaughter Nieve**

me because I am a parent giving another parent a helping hand and am doing this because they want me to be there.

It is also a privilege working alongside all the other volunteers. Some of them I have known this past eleven years and with new volunteers coming on board regularly we all get to know one another very well. Along with the valuable training we get we also have great CRAIC and indeed, if needed, there is always a shoulder to cry on! Behind every successful bunch of volunteers is a brilliant organiser.

Right now I feel I have come full circle. My own family is getting bigger every year. Along with my own five children, three of whom have partners, I now have three beautiful grandchildren.

My family knows I am always here for them. They know how lucky we all are to have our extended family within five minutes of each other. They realise also that everyone is not as lucky. Unlike our family there are families out there who can't cope, who feel lonely and alone and worst of all isolated – just how I felt 27 years ago when I arrived with my three-week-old twins and unfortunately Home-Start wasn't around then. Hopefully with more much needed volunteers, Home-Start will always be here and remain forever!

I'd never heard of Home-Start until a neighbour told me about this service for families who sometimes need a helping hand. Four children can be very demanding and exhausting and some days you dream about a little relief. My volunteer calls every Thursday afternoon and since her first visit she has helped out in more ways than I could have imagined. She takes the children to the park if I'm cleaning, she's cooked the dinner, minded the children whilst I've taken the eldest for a hospital appointment. In short, she's like an extension of the family. Home-Start is a wonderful help and with volunteers like mine it's a service with a smile!

# JOAN
## A MOTHER

## HOME-START
## CRAIGAVON

## A MOTHER

## HOME-START
## CAUSEWAY

I'd just had my second child when I was introduced to Home-Start. I was overwhelmed by the fact that she was suffering from kidney problems just like my other child. I felt I could not cope and became depressed. I had no help from my in-laws and no support. I did not live near my own family and felt totally alone. I suffered from high blood pressure after having a caesarean section with my daughter. When I heard about the idea that someone would come and visit me from Home-Start I was very nervous and unsure at first.

When I met my Home-Start volunteer my children really took to her from the very start. She has become a special friend and has helped me keep hospital appointments, reassured me when faced with difficulties. We had a lot in common. She has listened to me about things I could not share with anyone. I feel she will always be a special friend even now we have ended with Home-Start. We keep in touch by phone and meet up from time to time.

Thank you for giving me a friend.

# "THE ONLY OTHER MAN WAS THE BUS DRIVER"
## ...A FATHER'S STORY

**Barry with his daughter Bayleigh (4)**

It all started for me on a Wednesday morning about a year ago. My wife and her friend persuaded me to go along to a Parent & Toddler group that was run by Home-Start. I took our youngest daughter. Although she was at nursery she loved the morning group. At first the other parents were wary of me. After all I was invading their 'space' and they really didn't know what to make of me. "What are you doing here? A MAN!!" The only other male there was the bus driver who collected everyone and brought them to the group.

After a few weeks attending the group, helping with the kids (sorry, children), making tea and talking to the parents, they finally accepted me as one of them. As each week passed I found myself going down that little bit earlier to help set up the play equipment for the children and making the pots of tea for the mums and even doing the dishes (rubber gloves provided)! I would even help out in the craft corner with the kids. I don't know who had more fun, the kids or myself. I looked forward to the little chats I had with the parents and realised that we had a lot in common. Topics and problems discussed ranged from nappy rash to teenage tantrums!

Personally I have learned a lot of new parenting skills and because of it I can be a better parent to all my children. After a while the parents asked why didn't I become a volunteer? So, after some thought and with the support of my family, I decided to take on the role. Our Home-Start

## BARRY, A VOLUNTEER.
## HOME-START ANTRIM

organiser gave me all the information I needed and after completing a nine-week course I was officially a Home-Start volunteer and was able to wear my badge and fleece with pride! I now have been accepted as an Honorary Mother into the group, HOORAY!

I feel that there are a lot of fathers out there who could get a lot from being involved with Home-Start, even just by going along, watching the interaction of their own children with others of their own age and having a cup of tea and a chat with the parents. There is a lot in the saying 'mother knows best!'

I'm glad that I can put something back into the community. I might not be able to bring massive changes or anything like it, but being there for parents on a Wednesday morning to lend a hand or an ear or help bring a smile, is for someone, a big thing. Home-Start made me think, and it has changed my life for the better.

Home-Start made me think, and it has changed my life for the better.

# "I WANTED TO BE A GRANNY TO THIS HOUSEHOLD"

**MARIE, A VOLUNTEER.
HOME-START
BALLYNAHINCH**

I used to live in the small village of Moneyreagh. I had lived there for 26 years and was known by everyone. I was active in village life and took part in the Girl Guide movement, ran an Irish dancing class, Community Services, the Gardening Society and was honorary treasurer of the local Action Cancer Group.

Coming to live on the outskirts of Ballynahinch was a culture shock. I was completely isolated and I was very lonely. I saw the premises of Home-Start beside the Super Value Shop and wondered what went on there…for some reason I thought it was a charity for people coming home from hospital. Then one day the Down Advertiser had a 'wanted' ad for Home-Start volunteers and I rang immediately. The group I trained with were lovely women of all ages who had all had great burdens in their lives and had survived; now we were reaching out to others to help them in their hour of need.

I have been matched with my family – mother, father and three lovely daughters. I have only been three times and each time I stay a bit longer. The mother and girls have clicked with me and apparently the father knows my husband whom he met in the course of work some years before. I wanted to be a granny to this household and help like a granny could. The mother lost her own mother when she was five years old and this gap needs a substitute now. I hope I am capable of filling this role.

Wednesday is the day that belongs to my family. As time goes on and my own family get used to me going out and about again I hope to go to the Mother and Toddler Groups on Tuesdays and Thursdays, taking my Home-Start family with me to give the mother time to herself. We must see how we progress slowly and surely, helping each other in this life's journey with God's Blessing.

...now we were reaching out to others to help them in their hour of need.

# "HOME-START CHANGED MY WHOLE LIFE AROUND"

**AMANDA, A MOTHER
AND VOLUNTEER.
HOME-START ANTRIM**

Amanda

There are a number of reasons why Home-Start became part of my life and I would have to start in Australia in 1966 when my mother died of cancer leaving my father with six children under 12 years old. I was six, my mother only 32. Our father, with the help of our eldest sister, looked after us for the first year. I know he tried his best but in 1967 we were separated and put into care. I was put into a Dr. Barnardos home with my two sisters. My youngest sister and two brothers were put into foster care. When I was nine my father disappeared and no trace has been found to this day. Most of my time with Dr Barnardos was brilliant. Only the last year was terrible. The house parents were abusing us, sexually and physically. The home closed and I lived with a wonderful family who fostered me.

When I was 17 I started work and finally moved into my own flat. About three months before my 18th birthday I met a man who was originally from Ireland, although he had left Ireland with his parents in the early 1970s when he was 13. We got married in 1979 and left Australia in 1981 to settle in Dublin. We had four children but our marriage broke up in 1984 and my husband went back to Australia and left me in Ireland. I met my second partner and we moved to Belfast. We got a Housing Executive house in Antrim and settled down. At the same time my ex-husband returned to Antrim and kidnapped our children and took them to Australia. My new partner and I coped as best we could and we had our own daughter.

Two and a half years ago I returned to Ireland after spending more than 40 years in England. I left as a teenager and returned an O.A.P (almost). In England I left behind wonderful friends and work colleagues, but the hardest thing was leaving my lovely family. I had lived next door to my daughter and her children and also her childminder. My son and his family lived a few hundred yards away. What a wrench.

When I came to Ireland and got the house and garden to my satisfaction, I found I had far too much time on my hands. After several visits to my doctor and various pills and potions we both decided I needed something to do. My doctor suggested Home-Start. I had never heard of it but I arranged a meeting and decided to give it a try. I began the training sessions, which I really enjoyed, and just before Christmas 2002 I joined my first family group at Home-Start Causeway in Coleraine.

I took to it like a duck to water, loved the children and the company. Then in the New Year, Ann, the Scheme manager, took me to meet my first family. I was nervous and excited; I got on really well with my "wee" mum and love her little boy to bits. Since then I have supported another family for a short while and at the moment I have got a mum, dad and five little girls so I'm certainly not bored that day. All I can say is thanks Ann for accepting me into your team – you have saved my sanity.

# MAUREEN
## A VOLUNTEER

## HOME-START
## CAUSEWAY

**Amanda at a Home-Start family group**

For quite some time we were happy, as much as we could be and I did my best to cope with the loss of my oldest four children. As time went on my partner began to drink heavily. My health and our relationship deteriorated gradually over a number of years and when I was pretty bad with fibromialgia my health visitor asked me if I would like help from Home-Start. My youngest two children were under three and also one of my children in Australia had been killed in a hit and run accident.

Sadly my relationship with my partner ended and I moved out with our children. Home-Start has already given me great support and help in a number of ways and asked me if I would like to do one of their courses for self-awareness. It was during this course someone said to me that they thought I would be a good volunteer because of all I'd been through and I would understand mums and dads who had gone through similar things. So I did the next volunteer course and have learnt so much about myself and other people.

I really enjoy being part of Home-Start. I work with brilliant volunteers and our parent and toddler group and also with two families. I am very lucky to be a part of such a wonderful family because that is what Home-Start is all about and I am so grateful to them for they have changed my whole life around.

# A MOTHER

## HOME-START CARRICKFERGUS

I started having a volunteer because I was diagnosed with MS and needed some help with my children while my husband was working.

Over the past three years we have had three volunteers, who each had their own special qualities and talents and enriched our family life. Angela, Michelle and Lillian all got on well with us and were happy to do whatever I suggested, from painting to watching videos.

Sometimes when Lillian is here she will mind the boys while I lie down for an hour and the boys are very happy to be with her.

Home-Start has helped us a lot as a family in different ways. The different volunteers have been first class and have been very supportive of us.

Not only the volunteers but also Anne and Helen at the local Scheme have been great. We have also enjoyed parties, a day trip and received a hamper and presents…all because we were a Home-Start family. At the events it was good to meet committee members and also other families.

So Home-Start has, I feel, made a big difference to our family. At times, when I was very low, Stephen was still able to go out to work because a volunteer was coming. I appreciated their companionship and practical help and the boys had, and still have, a ball.

The relationships with the volunteers was and is good, I still keep in touch with my former volunteers and my present volunteer, Lillian, feels like a favourite auntie.

# "I THOUGHT THERE WERE NO GOOD PEOPLE..."

**RUTH, A MOTHER.
HOME-START
CLOGHER VALLEY**

## My family were referred to Home-Start

Clogher Valley as we were new to the area and isolated. There was a lack of public transport and we had great difficulty getting our child to playgroup. Our other child was very ill and we were having ongoing difficulties in relation to that. We were referred to Home-Start by our Health Visitor. I hadn't heard of Home-Start before but learned that we could be supported by a volunteer.

Initially, I did not want to get involved with Home-Start as we had previous experience of multi-agency involvement and I did not want to tell our story again…over the past five years we would tell our story to professionals who were sympathetic but then could do nothing to help. I did not want to talk every time I fell ill. Siobhan at Home-Start assured me I did not have to go through everything but to say what I felt able to share. Up to this I never went out unless my husband was there. I was very depressed and my daughter was very unwell.

When the volunteer started to come and visit a lot of things were happening and she was always there to listen and to talk. Our volunteer was very supportive, she faithfully came every week and she seemed like a nice girl. Gradually I got to know her and she could identify with our difficulties. On some visits we would go for a walk and other times go for a cup of tea and she also played with our granddaughter.

Home-Start was always there for us and very supportive. During this time there was a family crisis and Home-Start was there immediately. We had no family to listen. No one to listen but Home-Start. At the time we became involved with Home-Start I thought there were no good people and I did not trust people anymore. I regained my trust of people again. I feel I owe Home-Start a great deal as I would not have been able to cope. You helped immensely and I will always be thankful.

I am a divorced mother of five with a ten-year gap between the last two children. I found some spare time when the youngest started school and having done some volunteering in the past, decided to become a Home-Start volunteer. I ended up working for the local scheme. My life has become a lot fuller in various ways…meeting new friends, outings, gaining qualifications in First Aid, an NVQ in childcare. When I'm down-town and meet with some of the parents I've been with – who in the past didn't go out of the house – I get a good sense of achievement, so not only do families get a lot from Home-Start, I now have a much better understanding of family life.

**MARION**
A VOLUNTEER

HOME-START
NEWRY

# LINDA, A MOTHER.
## HOME-START CARRICKFERGUS

"Home-Start has been a great help to me because I have five small children and my partner used to be a long distance lorry driver. I was referred to Home-Start by my health visitor, Amber, from Carrick Health Centre because I was very depressed on my own with children. It was three years ago I was introduced to Dorothy, my Home-Start volunteer. She has been a great help to me, she is easy to talk to and we have developed a good friendship and she is very good to my children. I think Home-Start is a fantastic idea for parents with small children. "

# "I HAVE STARTED TO SEE A WAY FORWARD"

**EILIDH, A MOTHER.
HOME-START CRAIGAVON**

## My first introduction to Home-Start was in February 2003. Having one child at school and two children under two at home – both of whom were in and out of hospital regularly in 2003 – was stressful enough. But I also had physical health and mobility problems following the birth of my daughter and we had only recently moved to Lurgan. I knew nobody, my family were in Scotland and my husband could give little support.

My marriage broke down and my husband consequently left the family home in May 2003. Bernie, my Home-Start volunteer during this time has been a tower of strength for me. She has supported me in a practical way with the children…letting me feed the baby while she entertained Murray, coming to the doctor or hospital appointments to help with the children.

Lately she has been great when I needed emotional support and enables me to spend time with my older daughter, who was feeling I had little time for her and was always busy with the baby or at hospital. Through Home-Start and Bernie I have started to see a way forward. The children love having Bernie here and I look at Bernie as a friend whom I can talk to about anything in a non-judgemental way. She gives opinions and advice in a reassuring way and lets me talk things through to come to my own conclusion. She has played a very big part in helping me establish a strong family unit even without a partner.

# "HERE WE GO AGAIN – ANOTHER PERSON TELLING ME HOW TO RUN MY LIFE"

**MARIE, A MOTHER.**
**HOME-START NEWRY**

I was referred to Home-Start five years ago by my Child Care Social Worker because my life was in a mess. At that stage, I was a recovering drug addict with attitude – not just a chip but also a brick on my shoulder. I hated the world. I have three children, then aged nine, five and two, and all had been in foster care for a period. I had split with my husband – the father of my oldest child – and with the father of the two younger children, and was trying to manage on my own. I was very angry and very, very few people could get through to me. I was really involved with Social Services and they were all rubbing me up the wrong way. When the volunteer came I felt 'here we go again – another person trying to tell me how to run my life'. I remembered Ann coming, from the very first visit we got on – I liked her.

One of the things we recalled recently was my son sitting in the living room saying 'If I won a million pounds I would give some to my Mum, some to my brother and sister and…' then he stopped – he couldn't say Dad – because I would have gone off on one of my rants. I couldn't forgive his father for the things he had done to both of us but slowly Ann helped me see things from my son's point of view; this was his Dad.

Ann had a gentle way, an honest way of talking to me so that I could take things from her that when other people said them I got very angry. Ann had no ulterior motive – she had nothing to gain, I wasn't just a number. Others seemed to make little of my life story, Ann never did.

I shouted and ranted and raved with other services, but not with Ann. She brought me back down to earth – when she left after a visit I felt a weight lifted off my shoulders. She didn't judge me, didn't looked down her nose at me but when I was doing something wrong, she told me.

My children loved Ann. She read stories, talked to them, made a big fuss of them and they couldn't wait to tell her everything that had happened during the week. One of the things I remember Ann saying was "you never know when you are making a memory". She helped me look at life from my children's point of view. Ann also helped me practically; we would clear up the dishes together and talk. Sometimes I saw her twice a week or we talked on the phone. When I was in crisis I tortured her and she was always there for me. I felt that neither I, nor my children, were in a text book, but other people treated me like a text book case – Ann cared.

I got help with anger management, which Ann persuaded me to do. That helped – my therapist didn't talk down to me – I'm the one with the degree in life, I couldn't cope with people who had all the answers. I had too much hate in my life, I was obsessed with it without realising it and everyone suffered including me. I thought because of what HE had done I was justified.

It was a slow journey – I can't pinpoint when the change took place, but all of a sudden, my ex didn't affect me anymore. I can now look back and remember a lot of bad things, but they don't hurt the same.

I went back to college and now I am in a full time job. I still have problems and have difficulties with my children from time to time. There is a lot of work still to be done, but I'm not constantly self destructing anymore. I feel a great sense of achievement. I have more money and we have a better quality of life: we are managing well. I am in the process of buying my house from the Housing Executive – I couldn't have imagined that ever happening. I thought that was for 'everybody else', not me.

Even though Home-Start officially stopped visiting me over two years ago because my youngest child was five, Ann and I were in contact regularly for a long time and now we see her at least every couple of months. She has helped make me the person I am now. She will always be a special person for us. She is closer to me than my own family and I value her opinion quicker than theirs. For my kids, "there's nobody like Ann", they still have so much to tell her every time they see her.

I am determined to learn what it takes to fix my family. My volunteer has known hardship also, she has "walked the walk" so I appreciate the love and care she gave me. Home-Start is not just a 'band-aid', it's like an antibiotic… you get the full course!

# …when she left after a visit I felt a weight lifted off my shoulders.

# PAT
## A VOLUNTEER

## HOME-START
## DOWN DISTRICT

The day I first 'met' Home-Start began like any other day, plenty of routine housework – something I do not particularly enjoy, housework to me being a necessary evil. I had just moved to live in Downpatrick (to retire) from a fairly hectic life in Birmingham. I do recall a strong feeling of not belonging, also of feeling lonely and isolated. I soon realised I had to do something about this – it was my problem alone. I found myself going into charity shops where the people had more time to talk to me and pass pleasantries…the occasional joke, the same helpfulness I found in the library and pharmacies.

As time went on I still felt I had too much time on my hands, I was getting restless. Then to my great surprise a message came via the grapevine to enquire whether I would be interested in voluntary work for an organisation called Home-Start. I was very excited at the prospect of being able to put into operation some of the many skills I had gathered during my forty years working in the U.K.

I really could not wait for Home-Start's visit to my home. Dr Claire Magennis came to see me and together we went through the role of a Home-Start volunteer – the responsibilities and the overall need for professionalism at all times. The next step was a course of training which eventually led on to me being co-opted to the Management Committee of Home-Start Downpatrick.

What Home-Start has done for me is that it has enabled me to feel valued as a retired pensioner.

# "CARRYING TWO CHILDREN AT A TIME IS JUST NORMAL TO ME!"

**KRIS, A MOTHER.
HOME-START CRAIGAVON**

My name is Kris Armstrong and I am a mother of five children aged 5 and under. Caleb is 5, Rachel 3, Nathan 3, Sarah 17 months and Lois 17 months. Yes, there are two sets of twins! Having one set of twins is stressful enough but two is extra stressful, especially with them being close in age. Having said that, in some ways the recent set is easier than the first set, as I know what I'm up against. Carrying two children at a time is just normal to me!

As you can guess I am a stay-at-home mum, so I'm called on 24 hours a day. It's tiring and hard, especially when I can be up quite a few times during the night. I also lack family support as my husband's family lives over an hour away and my family lives in America. This makes my job all the harder.

I heard about Home-Start after the second set of twins were born. A social worker from our church gave us a form for self-referral. It was the best thing I could have done.

Deborah at the local Home-Start Scheme tries really hard to place the right volunteer with the right family. This is what makes this organisation so unique. As a mother you need someone else just to talk with, bounce ideas off and just befriend. Home-Start does this.

My current volunteer Dolores is wonderful and the kids adore her. I look forward to her coming every Monday, as they do. She comes in and gets stuck right in to whatever she sees needs doing. She has come to the doctor's surgery with me, entertained the kids while I get some things done, makes lunch and helps me make the tea for that night, plus many other things. She's the perfect volunteer for my situation.
The kids also do things for her that they wouldn't do for me, like wear big girl/boys pants and sit on the potty! I had been trying this for months and they just responded to her approach!

I would recommend Home-Start to anyone. It is the most reliable volunteer organisation I have ever had contact with.

# "I COULDN'T BELIEVE SHE HAD TAKEN THE TROUBLE TO FIND ME"

## HOW A YOUNG MOTHER TURNED THE TABLES ON A HOME-START VOLUNTEER

**When I joined Home-Start** in September 2001 my aim was to help someone who couldn't see light at the end of the tunnel. Well, did I expect a twist in the tale?!

I had a great time training to be a volunteer. I met some really nice people and felt good about myself because I was helping. I really hit it off with my 'mum'; She thought she wouldn't be able to communicate with other adults. She thought she had lost all her social skills being a mother of three – two of them being 6-month-old twins who didn't know the meaning of the word 'sleep'.

She was very wrong. She was a very intelligent articulate person. My role was to let her sleep. That happened once. We had some great chats. She was a very interesting funny girl with lots of stories of her homeland. I looked forward to our chats. I think she did as well. We became friends. She was battling her way through postnatal depression and sleep deprivation. The PND I could empathise with, having been there. I gave her hope.

## A VOLUNTEER.
## HOME-START CARRICKFERGUS

As well as being a Home-Start volunteer I was back holding down a nursing job and got a promotion, as well as being a mum of two. Then things changed! I needed gall bladder surgery. I wasn't recovering. I was very sick. I couldn't visit. I was PREGNANT! I couldn't eat or cook!

My Home-Start Mum didn't know where I lived but she knew the general area. She came looking for my car. I was sick, tired and tearful the day she called with the twins. I couldn't believe she had taken the trouble to find me. We chatted and she left. She returned a couple of hours after with a homemade lasagne, a homemade trifle and hot dogs for the kids. She knew I couldn't cook for the family. I cried I was so touched. I was the one who was supposed to be supporting her not the other way around. She called regularly after that. Now my 'mum' is smiling and managing the building of her own house.

Home-Start has had a very big impact in my life. I cannot visit at present due to my own family's commitments but I like to help in other ways. It has changed my life as a volunteer. What has it done for the families it supports?!

# "...A GOOD CAREER, NICE HOUSE AND KIND HUSBAND. WHAT HAD I TO BE DEPRESSED ABOUT?"

I had seen the adverts for Home-Start volunteers in the newspaper but knew nothing about the organisation. I have depression and I desperately wanted to get better. So I phoned asking if someone would come out to see me. At the time I felt that it would be just another thing that was advised by the health profession that sounded a good idea but would fail in practice.

Looking back now, I can say that it was the turning point in my illness. I had felt isolated with no friends and little family support. Depression had left me feeling that I could not function as a person. I had a young family – my children and husband trying to come to terms with my illness. I was a professional person with a good career, nice house and kind husband. What had I to be depressed about? I think it was the combination of guilt at working long hours and not spending enough time with the children, and postnatal depression after my fourth child which left me feeling that I could not leave the house, look after the children or even myself.

My volunteer had also had severe depression like me but was well on the road to recovery. When I saw how well she was able to cope with her life it made me realise that I could get better and have a normal life. Most importantly, if I said how I was feeling or what I found difficult, she could understand as she had been through the same.

## MARY, A MOTHER.
## HOME-START NEWRY

It made me feel that I wasn't on my own, that someone understood what I was going through. We would go shopping, go out for lunch or she would come to the house for a chat. Before, I took no regard to how I looked and felt that I didn't deserve to look after myself. My volunteer coming with me to shop gave me the confidence to go out and feel it was okay to do something just for myself. It made me realise how good it made me feel and when I got home I could deal with the family much better.

Home-Start has given me a new realisation that there are kind, decent people who are willing to help and show kindness, not pity. Taking time out of their own lives to help make someone else's life that bit better. I can't express in words how much Home-Start and my volunteer helped me come to terms with my illness. If anyone is thinking of using Home-Start, all I can say is that it is a practical, worthwhile service that can improve your life and most importantly the life of the children and family.

It made me feel that I wasn't on my own, that someone understood what I was going through.

# "WE COOK, SING, TALK, PLAY, READ, ENCOURAGE ...AND LISTEN"

**A VOLUNTEER.
HOME-START ARDS,
COMBER & PENINSULA**

## What does a volunteer do? It's a question I'm often asked. Well – we visit young mums in their own homes. They talk, we listen. We take them out to shops, doctor's appointments, dentists, child psychologists, speech therapists – the list is endless.

We play with the kids and encourage Mum to relax and join in.
We take Mum and kids out to drink coffee or drink coffee or tea at home.
We go on family outings.
We trawl the charity shops for nice clothes for the kids – and sometimes ourselves as well!
We help at birthday parties.
We go to the seaside in the summer.
We help bath and groom the dog.
We help clear out the cupboards (it's too big a job on your own if you are a Mum with under fives).
We have been known to help with decorating and gardening.
We make bonfires for Halloween.
We sew on buttons, replace elastic and sometimes shorten curtains or make cushions.
We cook, involving the kids if possible.
We help bath babies or change nappies.
We push swings and roundabouts for kids in the park.

We plant bulbs for Mummy for Christmas.
We make dough and play with it.
We're very talented artists (in the eyes of the children!).
We make things out of junk.
We sing and read stories.

## GET THE PICTURE?

I have been a volunteer with Home-Start for over fifteen years. It all began when I was asked to join the Steering Group when the Scheme was being set up, which led to being on the Management Committee. In order to understand my management role better I took volunteer training. Little did I know what I was letting myself in for – at one stage I was supporting seven families!

Before working with Home-Start I had been a Primary School teacher, I had run a pre-school playgroup and gone on to be a tutor with NiPPA – the Early Years Organisation. I had also fostered two long-term foster children who grew up with my own family. It was obvious that any voluntary work I undertook would be with children. As a result of being a home visitor I have somehow acquired many extra daughters – a few extra sons-in-law and many, many extra grandchildren. I suppose the main advantage of all this is that my own children all live a long way away – two in England, one in New Zealand – so I can hone my grand parenting skills on all these "extras" and I hope it keeps me up to date with what goes on in the world of young children and with the problems my own children have with their families. It is just wonderful to have such a large extended family.

Some years ago I visited a family in Ballywalter. There were two school-aged children, a lonely Mum and a toddler. What I felt we needed was to join a mother and toddler group but the Home-Start one was a long way away and in the afternoon my lonely Mum was collecting school-children and supervising homework. There wasn't a mother and toddler group in Ballywalter so we travelled to Kirkby. We all enjoyed it and everyone was very friendly but outside group hours we were five miles away.

So we sat down and hatched a plot to open a group in Ballywalter. My Mum was enthusiastic and mentioned it to other Mums at school as they were waiting to meet their children. Some were delighted to join us so we formed a committee, talked to NiPPA, opened a bank account with a seeding grant, eventually found premises and we opened. The group thrived and, although the original members have long since moved on, it is still thriving.

My lonely Mum's confidence increased with her involvement in the group.

When asked what Home-Start had done for her, her answer was simple – "Everything," she said.

My life changed in many ways in the year 2002. I had just had a baby when my husband's job was relocated. We had to move over 100 miles away, leaving all our family and friends. I began to feel extremely isolated and lonely in my new home. I knew no-one. On top of this I developed postnatal depression. Depression makes it virtually impossible to meet people and to socialise. I would stay at home and close all the curtains. I was becoming ever more isolated. The turning point came for me when I saw an advertisement in the newspaper for Home-Start. I knew I needed to reach out to someone, to break the cycle of loneliness that I had been trapped within.

I telephoned Home-Start and within a matter of days I was introduced to my Home-Start volunteer. I was apprehensive about letting a stranger into my home and my life, but I knew that I owed it to myself to give it a go.

Initially my volunteer provided emotional support. We would sit and talk, and when I was feeling down and didn't feel like talking, Mary, my volunteer, would talk for the both of us. For me that was the best bit, I was under no pressure to chat if I wasn't up to it. Two years on and my life has changed for the better. I no longer feel lonely, I have found a lifelong friend in my volunteer, my husband has a happier wife and my children have a contented mother.

# CLAIRE
## A MOTHER

## HOME-START NEWRY

# HOME-START SCHEMES IN NORTHERN IRELAND

**Home-Start in Northern Ireland**

Tel: **02890 460 772**

Fax: **02890 460 772**

E: **northernirelandoffice@home-start.org.uk**

W: **www.home-start.org.uk**

Antrim District

Ards, Comber & Peninsula Area (Greyabbey) (Newtownards)

Armagh & Dungannon (Moy)
  *Satellite: Armagh Outreach* (Moy)

Ballymena South

Ballynahinch

Blossom (Portadown)

Carrickfergus

Causeway (Coleraine)

Clogher Valley (Augher)

Colin/Lisburn (Belfast)

Colin/Lisburn (Lisburn)

Craigavon

Dalriada (Bushmills)

Down District (Downpatrick)

Dungannon Town

East Belfast

Irvinestown

Lakeland (Enniskillen)

Newcastle

Newry Central

Newry & Mourne (Newry)

Kilkeel

North Belfast

North Down (Bangor)

South Belfast

West Tyrone (Omagh)